# Contents

Joseph Walter of Bristol (1783-1856)
SHIPPING IN THE BRISTOL CHANNEL
Oil on canvas 66 × 90.2 cms
Private Collection
This picture belonged to Dr. D. Nicol who practised in Swansea in the early 19th
century.

# UNDER SAIL

## Swansea Cutters, Tallships and Seascapes 1830-1880

*A Glynn Vivian Art Gallery exhibition and publication, researched by*
*Dr. R. G. Howell, BM, FRCP.,* Honorary Curator of Art, Royal Institution of South Wales

SWANSEA CITY COUNCIL:

SWANSEA MUSEUM SERVICES

Copyright © Swansea Museum Services.

Published by the Glynn Vivian Art Gallery, Swansea City Council on the occasion of the exhibition 'Under Sail'
20 June–1 August 1987

ISBN  0  903189  23  2—Paperback
        0  903189  24  0—Hardback

Typeset and printed by D. Brown & Sons Ltd., Bridgend.

*Front cover*
James Harris
SHIP AND PILOT BOATS IN SWANSEA BAY
   WITH SINGLETON ABBEY IN THE BACKGROUND 1848
Oil on canvas 168 × 183 cms
Collection of the Rt. Hon. Lord Swansea
Signed Jas. Harris 1848. Probably James Harris' masterpiece.

*Title page*
James Harris
OFF THE GOWER COAST
Oil on canvas 97 × 152 cms
Collection of the Glynn Vivian Art Gallery
Signed.

*Back Cover*
James Harris
PICKING UP THE PILOT 1869   (Detail)
Oil on canvas 61.2 × 107.2 cms
Collection of the Glynn Vivian Art Gallery
Signed and dated. This picture is probably no. 149 in the 1902 catalogue, then the
property of Mrs. F. E. Williams and titled 'Mumbles Roads, with Shipping'.

THE GUILDHALL, SWANSEA SAI 4PA

TELEPHONE 50821

I am delighted that the Museum Services has assembled together for the first time this unique record both of the work of the marine artists who were living and working in Swansea and their subject matter – the great age of sail which was an essential element of Swansea's past, for shipping contributed to her growth as a major commercial port and industrial centre on the Bristol Channel.

The Council is proud of the achievements and developments which have taken place in Swansea. Times have changed greatly and in order to continue to prosper this has regrettably meant that old skills are not required, and new skills have replaced them to meet the challenge of each age. Thus, the great sailing vessels with their romantic billowing white sails which stir the spirit are no longer to be seen sailing off the coast. It is only due to the artists who drew, and painted the boats for a ready market of people willing to acquire a piece of Swansea waters to adorn their walls, that we are able today to provide these detailed historic illustrations of a bygone era.

Please enjoy this volume. Dr. Howell's informative essay provides the background detail and the setting which contributed to the rise and demise of the wooden ship; he describes the unique features of the Swansea Pilot Cutters, the development of Swansea as a port and the rise and decline of the oyster beds. This book is profusely illustrated for it is the paintings and photographs which capture the spirit of the great age of sail.

Councillor H. W. Ayres
LORD MAYOR OF SWANSEA

Thomas Luny (1759-1837)
SHIP OFF SHAKESPEARE CLIFF
Oil on canvas 44.5 × 67.5 cms
Collection of Mr. & Mrs. F. B. Cockett
Luny worked for many years at Teignmouth
near Exeter.

William Van de Velde, the Younger (1633-1707)
SHIPPING IN BREEZY WEATHER
Oil on canvas 44.5 × 67.5 cms
Collection of Mr. & Mrs. F. B. Cockett
Dutch 17th century painters and especially
the Van de Velde family had great influence
on British Marine painters.

# Introduction

In 1957, David Bell, Curator of the Glynn Vivian Art Gallery, wrote 'In Swansea there was in the middle of the 19th century a little school of amateur marine painters of considerable competence. Today they are almost forgotten.... The most accomplished of these was James Harris (1810-1887), a marine painter in oil of great skill, but little known today, even in Swansea.'

Since then the increased interest in marine painting has included James Harris, but he is regarded as a rare artist and little is known of his background.

David Bell was not strictly correct when he wrote of a 'school of marine painters'. The contemporaries of James Harris working in the Swansea area were very varied in their art, and they can only be brought together in the sense that they all play a part in the James Harris story.

Nor were they amateurs. Even Calvert Jones, the wealthy clergyman and artist, was not above being involved in the commercial exploitation of calotype photography organised by Henry Fox Talbot.

It is now 85 years since a large number of James Harris' works were brought together in Swansea at the Royal Institution of South Wales in 1902. The first exhibition showing the works of the Rev. Calvert Jones was held at the Glynn Vivian Gallery in 1973.

This publication assembles together for the first time all those artists who made a contribution to marine painting in Swansea between 1830 and 1880, and is a visual record of the exhibition 'Under Sail' which was shown at the Glynn Vivian Art Gallery, Swansea, 20 June-1 August 1987.

# Background

The period 1830-1880 covers the development of Swansea from the small tidal harbour at the mouth of the river Tawe into a large commercial port which was required to meet the needs of the metallurgical industry which developed in Swansea. The West Pier was built in about 1800, followed in 1805-1810 by the East Pier, which enclosed Fabian's Bay. The river was navigable up to Landore, providing access to the Hafod Copper Works and the Cambrian Pottery. Further developments such as New Cut in 1845, South Dock in 1859 and the Prince of Wales Dock in 1882, with the opening of the South Wales Railway to Swansea in 1850, reflect the rapid industrial development in the 19th century.

Although trade from Swansea was world wide, the public imagination has been captured by the feats of the ships and their crews which brought copper ore from Chile, round Cape Horn, for smelting in Swansea. The Cape Horners, both ships and men, are part of Swansea's folk memory.

A number of the Portraits of the ships, which traded out of Swansea, have survived and they accurately record the nautical detail and personality of each vessel.

Early pictures of Swansea often show the tidal harbour with the West and East Piers, but as the docks developed our artists turned their backs on the Industrial Revolution and sought more agreeable subjects in Gower. Indeed, they also more or less ignored the development of steam. A steam pacquet service between Swansea and Bristol began in 1823, the paddle boat Glamorgan taking eight hours for the journey in each direction. By 1880, of the 5366 ships which used the docks in that year, 1547 were steamers.

We know that Calvert Jones was interested in steam powered battleships in the Mediterranean in 1850-1860, but in the Harris exhibition of 1902, only one picture, 'A steam ship off the Mumbles Lighthouse' by James Harris, paid recognition to the decline of sail power.

SWANSEA HARBOUR _c._1830
   WITH THE STEAM PACKET GLAMORGAN
Aquatint, published by T. Bedford, High Street, Bristol 24.3 × 83 cms
Collection of the Glynn Vivian Art Gallery
The Glamorgan was the first steam ship to enter Swansea, built 1823 for service
between Swansea and Bristol. The engines were built by Price & Co., Neath. On her
first visit to Swansea the 'Glamorgan' steamed up the river Tawe to Vivian & Sons,
Hafod Copper works.

Newman & Co.
VIEW OF SWANSEA *c*.1860
Lithograph 22 × 32.5 cms
Private Collection
Published by W. Palmer, Swansea. Shows the New Cut, the Railway Station and the
Pottery.

Alexander K. Brander
LANGLAND OF SWANSEA, CAPTAIN JOHN GEORGE 1882
Oil on canvas 53.5 × 84 cms
Private Collection
Registered at Swansea no. 70497, 639 Tons. Built at Middlesborough in 1875. Barque
rigged. In 1881 owned by William Henry Tucker of Swansea and in 1890 was
managed by Joseph W. Simpson.

School of Samuel Walters of Liverpool
ZETA
Oil on canvas 81.4 × 135 cms
Owned by Henry Bath & Son Limited
Built at Glasgow by Alexander Stephen in 1865, owned by Henry Bath & Son of
Swansea. This was the first sailing vessel in Swansea to be fitted with a steam
auxiliary. By 1872 she had been sold and renamed Urmeneta of Valparaiso.

James Harris
VIEW OF THE HAFOD COPPER WORKS
  FROM THE EAST SIDE OF THE RIVER TAWE
Oil on canvas 86.5 × 138.3 cms
Collection of the Glynn Vivian Art Gallery
This interesting picture shows activities along the River Tawe *c.*1850. The smoke of
the Hafod Copper works can be seen in the distance, and also the kilns of the Pottery.
Coal is being loaded into ships in the middle foreground. Signed.

W. H. Yorke
SUMATRA OF LLANELLY, D. THOMAS MASTER
Oil on canvas 49.4 × 74.2 cms
Private Collection
Reg. no. 77063. 721 Tons. Built at Sunderland in 1866. Barque rigged. Registered at
Llanelly, owned by Thomas Roberts, Gwalia House, Llanelly.

E. Adam
SKETTY BELLE OF SWANSEA, THOMAS MENDUS
   COMMANDER, OFF CAPE LA HÈVE 1877
Oil on canvas 60 × 90 cms
Private Collection
A Brigantine of 171 Tons. Built by Pierce Lebé at Quebec, May 1866. Originally
owned by William Colqin of Carlisle, but was registered at Swansea. By 1879 she had
been sold to L. Tullock of Swansea and was eventually with owners in Freemantle,
Australia as a supply ship to the Pearl Fishing Fleet in Torres Straights.

Anon
THUNDERBOLT
Oil on canvas 66 × 103 cms
Private Collection
Built in 1863 by Samuelson and owned by Burgess & Co. Swansea, with T. Mendus,
master 1890-93. She was lost on 3 November 1893 on Hartwell Reef, Bonavista, Cape
Verde. Ten men drowned. Captain Mendus had left ship with fever, in South
America, and the ship was lost on the next outward voyage.

Alexander K. Brander
ILLIMANI OFF THE MUMBLES
Oil on canvas 59 × 90.2 cms
Collection of Burgess & Co. Ltd., Swansea
Iron ship. Barque rigged. Built in 1875 by Dobies of Glasgow. 630 Tons Gross.
Owned by J. E. Burgess, Swansea. She was almost destroyed by a tidal wave off
Oquique, Chile.

Anon
HERBERT 1867
Oil on canvas 49.5 × 76 cms
Collection of Burgess & Co. Ltd., Swansea
Barque rigged. Flies the Norwegian Flag and Burgess House Flag.

# Pilot Cutters

Pilot Cutters were small vessels used to take a pilot out to the large ships to guide them safely to harbour. Marine artists, like painters of horses and hunting scenes, suffer from a shortage of possible subjects. Pilot Cutters are therefore frequently included in marine paintings as they provide a variety of subject matter and interest when either approaching or returning from a ship, and give a sense of activity to a painting.

*The Swansea Pilot Cutters* had certain unique features which make a Swansea seascape immediately recognisable even in the absence of landscape. The Swansea pattern of cutters were two masted schooners with an exaggerated rake of the main mast. The sails were laced directly to the mast without rings. The gaffs were very short and there were no shrouds. These features were designed to facilitate the pilot cutters, so they could easily draw alongside a ship.

The early boats, up to 1860, were 20-30 feet long and the later boats from 1860-1895 were 40-50 feet and decked. In 1898 the steam cutter 'The Beaufort' replaced the sailing boats.

The Swansea Pilot cutters were named and numbered as follows:

*Boats in service 1840-1860*

| 1 | Singleton | 6 | Sarah |
|---|-----------|----|-----------|
| 2 | Tom Rosser | 7 | Neptune |
| 3 | Zion | 8 | Henry |
| 4 | Faith | 9 | Providence |
| 5 | Swanzey | 10 | Vivian |

*The Larger decked boats up to 1895*

| 1 | Vivian | 7 | Alarm |
|---|----------|----|-------------|
| 2 | Vigilant | 8 | TWT |
| 3 | Rival | 9 | Grenfell |
| 4 | Benson | 10 | Camilla |
| 5 | Lizzie | 11 | Charles Bath |
| 6 | Glance | | |

A number of paintings record local detail such as the oyster skiffs and dredges. The Oyster industry in Swansea Bay goes back to Roman times, but it was during the 19th century that it reached its peak and then declined. By 1850 there were 400 people employed and in 1860 there were 200 skiffs and 1000 people earning a living from the industry.

In earlier days open rowing boats were used to drag the oyster dredges, but from 1850, 4 to 5 ton sailing skiffs were used, each with a crew of three.

Heavy dredges removed the oysters from the sea bed and were winched into the skiff. The oysters were then returned to the water, until ready for sale, in oyster 'perches'. These were divisions of the foreshore, roughly marked out by stones and wooden markers.

Excessive dredging depleted the oyster beds and although the industry continued up to 1914, decline set in during the last quarter of the 19th century, leading to much hardship among the people of the village of Mumbles to the west of the City of Swansea.

MODEL OF THE PILOT CUTTER GRENFELL S9
Collection of Swansea Yacht and Sub-Aqua Club
The Grenfell was built at Swansea by Philip Bevan in 1865. Length 50ft, beam 13ft, draught 8ft. When the steam pilot cutter 'Beaufort' was introduced in 1898, Grenfell was retained as a reserve vessel. She was sold to Bristol as a hulk in 1904.

James Harris
PILOT CUTTER IN STORMY SEA *c.*1860
Oil on canvas 29 × 44.5 cms
Collection of the Royal Institution of South Wales.

James Harris
PILOT CUTTERS RACING *c*.1855
Oil on canvas 34.5 × 52 cms
Collection of Edward and Charles Harris
Signed.

James Harris
TAKING ON THE PILOT, OFF MUMBLES HEAD
Oil on canvas 26.5 × 44.5 cms
Private Collection
Signed.

James Harris
PICKING UP THE PILOT *c.*1870
Oil on canvas 43 × 74 cms
Collection of Edward and Charles Harris

James Harris
SHIP WITH PILOT BOAT OFF SWANSEA HARBOUR
Oil on canvas 59 × 89 cms
Private Collection
Signed.

James Harris Jnr.
TWO PICTURES OF BOATS ON SHORE
    WITH OYSTER DREDGES
Watercolour 19 × 47.5 cms each
Collection of Edward and Charles Harris

# James Harris
# (1810-1887)

James Staden Harris died on June 19th 1887, aged 77, at Reynoldston, Gower, where he had lived at Bryn House since 1882. His widow Emma died on February 19th 1890, and they are buried in Reynoldston churchyard.

An obituary in the *Cambrian* newspaper of July 1st 1887 and a further report in *The South Walian*, a local monthly newspaper, in December 1902, provide biographical information which may be summarised as follows:

*1810*   Born at Exeter.

*1828*   The Harris family moved to Swansea and set up a business as Carvers and Gilders of picture frames in Wind Street. The family consisted of John Harris, his wife, two sons and a daughter. James was the elder son.

*1830*   The Swansea Directory lists John Harris as a carver and gilder in Wind Street.

*1836*   John Harris died on 12.2.1836, aged 58, and the family carried on the business.

*1842*   An advertisement in the *Cambrian* newspaper (1.10.1842) is in James Harris' name, working from 40 Wind Street.

*1846*   On 15.8.1846 his mother married again, to Mr. D. Herring of Barnstable, at St. Mary's Swansea, and one week later at St. Mary's, on 22.8.1846, his sister Sarah married John Waring Jones. It is probable that James' interest in the business ended at this time.

*1849*   Hunt's *Directory* lists James Harris as an artist, living at Mumbles.
John Waring Jones is described as a Carver, Gilder and picture frame maker in Wind Street.

*1850*   In Hunt's Directory James Harris is again listed as an artist living at Mumbles.
John Waring Jones is listed as Carver & Gilder at 29 Wind Street.
It has been said that the Harris family set up

business in 1828 at 40 Wind Street when they settled in Swansea. The first definite evidence of this is the advertisement in 1842, 14 years later. After his sister's marriage in 1846, her husband John Waring Jones is described in 1849 as a Carver and Gilder. In 1850 he is listed as working from 29 Wind Street and in 1854 he is not recorded. There is probably much to learn about the apparent lack of fortune in this business.

*1869*   Pearce Brown's Directory lists James Harris as a marine artist, living at Underhill Cottage Oystermouth. This house has not been identified.

*1882*   He moved to Reynoldston, living at Bryn House.

*1887*   He died aged 77 on 19.6.1887 leaving his widow Emma, two sons and three daughters. He was buried in Reynoldston churchyard.

*1890*   His widow Emma died on 19.2.1890. A single gravestone commemorates them both.

We know nothing of the Harris family in Exeter or why they migrated to Swansea in 1828. John Harris is said to have been a capable artist, and this talent was inherited by James, his elder son.

In addition to the instruction he would have received from his father, it is reasonable to suggest that while at Exeter James would have seen and been influenced by the works of the prolific marine artist Thomas Luny (1759-1837), who had moved from London to nearby Teignmouth in about 1807. He may also have seen the work of Joseph Walter of Bristol (1783-1856), now recognised as a major marine artist. However there is no obvious similarity to the work of any of the artists mentioned which cannot be attributed to the supreme influence which the Dutch 17th century artists, particularly the Van de Velde family, had made on British marine painting. In an undated manuscript concerning a proposed exhibition of pictures in Swansea among the Mansel papers is a note of 'a copy of Vandervelt by Harris Senior.'

In the 1830's the Rev. Calvert Richard Jones, the wealthy artist and pioneer photographer, introduced James Harris to the marine artist George Chambers (1803-1840), then working in London. It is assumed that Harris worked in Chambers' studio, probably financed by Calvert Jones. In recent years three paintings by Chambers dated 1836 and 1838 of Swansea scenes have been identified, and as the introduction to Chambers by Calvert Jones is noted in Harris's obituary immediately after his death, these facts are probably correct.

Sale catalogues of the contents of great houses in the Swansea area, and present ownership, show that the Vivian, Talbot, Llewellyn and Bath families all of whom were of significant influence in South Wales patronised Harris, although the description of the pictures is often too vague to identify them accurately. C. R. M. Talbot of Margam commissioned him to paint pictures on a voyage round the Horn, and Harris sailed in the Chelydra, a 500 ton ship built at Newport in 1838 for the opium trade in China and fitted for passengers.

Talbot was a frequent visitor to the Mediterranean in a series of steam yachts which he owned. There is no record of Harris ever accompanying him, although Calvert Jones, who was more of Talbot's social class and a close personal friend, was frequently included. Perhaps the picture of shipping off Messina by James Harris (now in the Glynn Vivian Art Gallery collection) was painted from sketches by Calvert Jones?

Ship portraits were popular with owners and masters. A Swansea butcher and ship owner, William Jenkins commissioned Harris to paint The Agnes Blakey, The Alicia, The Emperor of China and The Rajah of Sarawak.

James Harris exhibited in London thirteen pictures at the Suffolk Street Gallery and three at the British Institution. In December 1902 at the 14th annual exhibition of the Swansea Art Society at the Royal Institution of South Wales there was a loan exhibition of 64 paintings by 'the late James Harris' and 39 watercolours and 'Black and White' by his son, James Harris Junior. There was also a 'Coast Scene' by John Harris, and a portrait of James Harris, owned by Mr. Alfred Hall, which regrettably cannot be traced. There is now no recorded likeness of James Harris. Family tradition says that James Harris was short and stocky with a fresh complexion and blue eyes.

The 1902 Exhibition catalogue is tantalising in that the description of the pictures is minimal and sizes are not given. Only 6 or so can now be identified with certainty. 'Black and White' pictures are listed as being by James Harris, Junior, but it seems that they were by his father. These works are mentioned as 'charcoal pictures' in James Harris's obituary of 1887, and said to be very popular. They are probably the small sepia pictures, painted with an opaque medium on paper and signed 'Harris' which are painted in the manner of an oil painting, and are finished works, not sketches.

It is probable that Edward Duncan (1803-1882) was the last and most significant influence on James Harris. A pencil sketch of a Mumbles oyster ketch, signed Edward Duncan and dated 1839, is the earliest indication of Duncan working in South Wales. It marks the beginning of a love affair with Gower carried on by the Duncan family for over 100 years, until the death a few years ago of his two granddaughters, who lived at Horton.

Edward Duncan's sons Lawrence, Edward, Allen and Walter were all painters and the Harris and Duncan families became close friends.

They painted the same subjects, such as The Worms Head from the Sea, which is known in oils by James Harris and Edward Duncan and in watercolour and oils by James Harris Junior. There is a photograph of a lost 'View of Oystermouth from the Sea', by Harris and Duncan. In Duncan's studio sale after his death there were five pictures by James Harris in his personal collection.

James Harris
SHIP PREPARING TO SAIL, SWANSEA BAY
Oil on canvas 71 × 106.5 cms
Collection of the Rt. Hon Lord Swansea
Signed J. Harris, 1851(?)

Duncan realised that dark stormy pictures were out, and the market for ship portraits was limited. The rising middle classes required bright cheerful pictures of recognisable scenes.

So James Harris, who had started out in the 18th century style, where man battled against the elements for small returns, by about 1860 had become a Victorian painter. His pictures were brighter, the landscape element more prominent and people were shown actively enjoying themselves.

Within these styles of painting there runs a common thread. That is the quality of his painting of ships, with the accurate detail of a miniaturist and a particular sculptural quality of the sails, which together with a high standard of figure painting, and an ability to capture atmosphere and light, lifts his work into the highest class.

James Harris
SHIPPING IN STORMY WEATHER *c.*1850
Oil on canvas 30 × 41 cms
Collection of Mr. & Mrs. F. B. Cockett

James Harris
THREE MASTED BARQUE OFF THE GOWER COAST
Oil on canvas 68.5 × 106.5 cms
Private Collection

James Harris
OYSTER BOATS PASSING BETWEEN THE ISLANDS
  AT THE MUMBLES
Oil on canvas 30.5 × 55.9 cms
Collection of the National Library of Wales
Post 1860.

James Harris
INNER SOUND, THE MUMBLES
Oil on canvas 30.5 × 55.9 cms
Collection of the National Library of Wales
Post 1860.

James Harris
SHIPPING OFF THE MUMBLES
Oil on canvas 30.5 × 56 cms
Private Collection
Signed.

James Harris
MUMBLES LIGHTHOUSE ON A CLEAR DAY
Oil on canvas 30.5 × 56 cms
Private Collection
Signed.

James Harris
OYSTERMOUTH FROM THE SEA *c.*1860
Oil on canvas 60 × 106.5 cms
Collection of the Royal Institution of South Wales
The Christadelphian Chapel, dated 1850 is still standing.

James Harris
SWANSEA BAY IN STORMY WEATHER
Oil on canvas 70.3 × 89.5 cms
Collection of the Royal Institution of South Wales
Signed J. Harris 1834, the earliest dated work.

James Harris
THREE MASTED BARQUE OFF THE MUMBLES *c.*1850
Oil on canvas 58.5 × 89 cms
Private Collection
Signed.

James Harris
SHIP IN SWANSEA BAY WITH FIGURES ON ROCKS
Oil on canvas 73.5 × 104 cms
Private Collection
Signed. Dated post 1860. Ship flies the Henry Bath & Son houseflag.

James Harris
SHIP AND PILOT BOAT IN A STORM
Oil on canvas 15 × 19 cms
Private Collection

James Harris
BRIGANTINE RUNNING BEFORE A BREEZE
Oil on canvas 12.5 × 21 cms
Collection of Dr. D. J. Harris.

James Harris
ON THE ROCKS *c*.1865
Oil on canvas 15 × 25 cms
Private Collection

James Harris
TWO MASTED SHIP OFF MUMBLES *c.*1850
Oil on canvas 43 × 81.2 cms
Private Collection

James Harris
SHIP DRESSED OVER ALL
Oil on canvas 40.5 × 67.5 cms
Collection of Edward and Charles Harris
This may be 'HMS Endeavour saluting in Swansea Bay'. no. 160 in the 1902 Harris
exhibition, but it possibly may be a merchant ship trading in the Far East and
permitted to carry guns.

James Harris
SHIPS IN CALM
Oil on canvas 29 × 44.5 cms
Collection of the Royal Institution of South Wales

James Harris
SHIPPING IN A CALM OFF MUMBLES
Oil on canvas 48.5 × 82.5 cms
Collection of Edward and Charles Harris

James Harris
SHIPS OFF OYSTERMOUTH
Oil on canvas 20.5 × 30.5 cms
Private Collection

James Harris
WORMS HEAD FROM THE SEA *c.*1870
Oil on canvas 60 × 106.5 cms
Private Collection
Probably no. 150 in the 1902 exhibition as being by John Syer of Bristol, with ships by
Harris.

Details from
picture opposite

James Harris
THREE MASTED BARQUE OFF THE MUMBLES *c.*1850
Oil on canvas 61 × 91.5 cms
Private Collection
Signed. The battery around the lighthouse was built in 1860, a useful marker in dating
paintings.

James Harris
BARQUES AT NIGHT IN ROUGH WEATHER
Oil on canvas 43 × 74 cms
Collection of the Glynn Vivian Art Gallery

James Harris
SMALL SEPIA PICTURES
Each signed. Painted with body
colour in the manner of oil
painting and are finished works.
Average 14 × 25 cms
Private Collection

James Harris
PILOT CUTTER IN STORMY WEATHER
Oil on board 15 × 25.5 cms
Private Collection

James Harris
SHIPS OFF MUMBLES *c*.1860
Oil on canvas 34 × 61 cms
Collection of the Royal Institution of South Wales

James Harris
SHIPS IN CALM WATER IN SWANSEA BAY *c.*1860
Oil on canvas 22 × 37 cms
Collection of the Royal Institution of South Wales

James Harris
SHIPS BETWEEN OYSTERMOUTH AND SWANSEA
Oil on board 15.2 × 25.5 cms
Private Collection
Signed. Old label on reverse: 'Bought Clyne Castle sale Nov. 1952. James Harris
Senior, View, Swansea Bay'.

James Harris
SHIPS OFF MUMBLES *c.*1870
Oil on canvas 24 × 44.5 cms
Collection of the Royal Institution of South Wales
Signed Harris.

James Harris
SHIP IN STORMY WEATHER *c*.1850
Oil on canvas 29 × 38.7 cms
Private Collection

James Harris
SHIPS RUNNING INTO SWANSEA HARBOUR *c*.1850
Oil on canvas 29 × 38.7 cms
Private Collection

James Harris
SHIPS IN ROUGH SEA *c.*1850
Oil on canvas 34 × 52 cms
Collection of the Royal Institution of South Wales

James Harris
PILOT CUTTER AND
 SHIP IN SQUALL
Oil on panel 12.7 × 24 cms
Collection of Edward and Charles Harris

James Harris
PILOT MAKING FOR SHIP
Oil on canvas 20.2 × 35.5 cms
Collection of Dr. D. J. Harris
Signed.

James Harris
SHIP IN DISTRESS, HOVE TO
Oil on canvas 33.5 × 19.5 cms
Collection of the Glynn Vivian Art Gallery

*Overleaf*
James Harris
PENCIL SKETCHES
Each Approx 14 × 30.5 cms
Private Collection
Very few examples of James Harris' sketchbook pages remain.

Mumbles Roadstead in an Easterly gale

68

Copper ore man reefed down off Snettook
James Harris Sen.

from a sketch done —

Light house before the fort was built
D. Harris Sen.

James Harris
THREE MASTED SHIP OFF MUMBLES
  WITH LIGHTHOUSE *c.*1850
Oil on canvas 60 × 90.4 cms
Private Collection

James Harris
SHIPPING IN THE CHANNEL 1870
Oil on canvas 60 × 106 cms
Private Collection

W. Adolphus Knell
SHIP OFF THE MUMBLES
Oil on canvas 44 × 74 cms
Collection of the Glynn Vivian Art Gallery
Attributed to W. A. Knell, but likely to be by James Harris.

James Harris
WORMS HEAD FROM THE SEA *c.*1870
Oil on canvas 29 × 54.5 cms
Private Collection
Signed.

# James Harris, Junior
# (1847-1925)

Photo reputed to be James Harris
Junior.

James Harris, Junior, was the eldest of James Harris' two sons and three daughters, and the only one of his generation to paint. Born in 1847, he grew up as a Victorian painter in watercolour, a medium seldom, if ever, used by his father. His infrequent work in oil is only occasionally successful. There is little doubt that he owed his training to Edward Duncan. In the Mansel Collection manuscript he is referred to as 'Harris, the younger, pupil of Duncombe', and like Duncan he started as a painter of ships and the sea and gradually evolved into a landscape painter. We are concerned here with his earlier work as a seascape painter.

James Harris, Junior, initially signed his work in full and often dated, perhaps until his fathers' death in 1887. An exception is that he painted some small watercolours, almost 'Impressionist' in style, which are signed J. HARRIS in capitals. Perhaps this was his gesture to French plein-air painting which was beginning to have influence in Britain in 1870-1880.

James Harris, Junior, died on December 11th 1925, aged 72 years, and was buried in Oystermouth Cemetery (Grave no. 4515) his epitaph being 'In the evening, it shall be light'.

As an associate member of Swansea Art Society, a classification open to professional artists, the Society's records give his address as follows.

1902-1910    *Reynoldston.* Perhaps he continued living here after the death of his mother in 1890.

1911-1912    *1 Castleton Place*, Mumbles.

1912    *8 Southwood Road, Ramsgate.* One of his sisters married George Stanfield Walters, a Thames Estuary marine painter, and this may have been her address.

1921    *Seacot, Limekiln Road, Mumbles.* This was the home of the Williams family with whom he lodged. Mrs. Emma Williams paid for his burial and grave.

He left at least seven sketchbooks, dating from April 1866 to May 1892. They are briefly described as follows:

(1)    *Undated*, but the Battery on Mumbles Head indicates after 1860. Mostly pencil sketches of local boats.

(2)    *April 1st, 1866.* Pencil sketches of local boats and occasional landscape in watercolour.

(3)    *June 1867.* 'Dordrecht'. June 1867. Watercolour sketches of canals, windmills and buildings with sailing barges.

(4)    *September 29th, 1867.* The most interesting. Sketches of coastlines, details of rigging etc. Describes a voyage from the Clyde, round Cape Horn. This sketchbook relates to a number of finished watercolours which are signed and dated.
The ship has been identified as the barque Eta, no. 51110, S. Grey, Master, owned by the Swansea firm Henry Bath & Son, and built by Charles Hill at Bristol in 1865. There are a number of paintings in existence which illustrate the voyage. The Eta left the Clyde on October 2nd 1867, rounded Cape Horn on December 7th, arriving at Valparaiso on December 22nd. On February 25th 1868 she sailed for Liverpool, arriving on May 26th 1868.

(5)    *July 5th, 1871.* Pencil sketches of local boats and figures. Included is a drawing of an artist at work. Could this be Harris Senior?

(6)    *October 2nd, 1880.* Sketches made on a voyage—Capetown on October 25th 1880, Ascension Island, Constantinople April 21st 1881. The pencil notes are difficult to read.

(7)   *May 1882*. Maritzberg, Natal. Mostly pencil drawings
      of trees and vegetation.

James Harris, Junior, is the nearest to us in time, but he
remains an elusive figure. A photograph of a bearded man
is reputed to be him, towards the end of his life, but we are
not certain.

No doubt he suffered the fate of so many others who follow
in the steps of a more famous father.

James Harris Jnr.
SHIPPING IN A CALM
Oil on canvas 20.2 × 30.5 cms
Collection of Neville and Rachel Douglas-Jones

James Harris Jnr.
ABOARD SHIP April 18/68
Watercolour 19 × 34.2 cms
Collection of A. J. Williams

James Harris Jnr.
SHIP OFF A MOUNTAINOUS COAST
Watercolour 27.2 × 47 cms
Private Collection
Signed J. Harris Jan 25 1868.

James Harris Jnr.
WHALING BOAT
Watercolour 27.2 × 47 cms
Private Collection

*Above*
James Harris Jnr.
OFF VALPARAISO 1868
Watercolour 11.25 × 33 cms
Private Collection
Signed J. Harris '68

*Below*
James Harris Jnr.
SHIP OFF THE HORN April 21/68
Watercolour 15.2 × 34.2 cms
Collection of A. J. Williams

James Harris Jnr.
HELVETIA IN DISTRESS UNDER WORMS HEAD 1887
SENDING MAN ASHORE BY BREECHES BUOY
Sepia 31.5 × 49 cms
Private Collection
Signed J. Harris Jnr.

*Helvetia* wrecked Rhosili Tuesday 1 November 1887

The Barque *Helvetia*, of Horten (Norway), Capt. Stevensen, was on passage from Campbellton, New Brunswick to Swansea. On the night of Monday 31 October she was off Mumbles making signals for a pilot but none came out. A fresh breeze came up from the south east and she was obliged to stand down channel. She drifted across the Helwick shoal where she lost part of her deck load and ran around Worms Head into Rhosili Bay. The Coastguard Lifesaving Apparatus Crew at Rhosili got a line over her and one man was brought ashore by the breeches buoy. The remaining members of the crew came ashore in their boats. At 5.30 p.m. she drove onto the sands where she became a complete wreck with her cargo scattered about the beach.

(The vessel's ribs may still be seen at Rhosili close to the highwater mark.)

James Harris Jnr.
WAVES BREAKING ON A ROCKY SHORE
Watercolour 29 × 48.5 cms
Private Collection

James Harris Jnr.
THE BARQUE ETA
Watercolour 30.5 × 50 cms
Private Collection
The Barque ETA, Reg. no. 51110 was owned by Henry Bath & Son of Swansea, but originally built at Bristol by Charles Hill in September 1865. Painting signed J. Harris Jnr. Oct 8 1867.

# George Chambers
# (1803-1840)

George Chambers was born of a poor family in Whitby, and began work on ships when only 8 years old. At 12 his artistic ability began to develop and he finished his seaman apprenticeship after only two years and returned to Whitby, where he worked as a house and ship painter for three years. In 1822 he went to London and was befriended by Christopher Crawford, the eccentric landlord of the 'Waterman's Arms' at Wapping, who encouraged his career. His work was seen in a dealer's window by Admiral Capel, and this led to introductions to influential clients and eventually to commissions from King William IV. Chambers' health deteriorated and he died at Brighton on October 29th 1840.

His connection with Swansea may have been through one of the wealthy Swansea industrialists, who were frequently in London society. However it could have been through his fellow Yorkshireman, Thomas Hornor, who worked from 1814 to 1820 painting panoramic views of gentlemen's estates in the Neath Valley. In 1824 Hornor started a project in Regents Park, with a rotunda consisting of 46,000 square feet of canvas painted with a panoramic view of London. Chambers worked on the panorama from 1825-1829 and consequently knew Hornor, who had a good knowledge of the Swansea locality.

George Chambers
PILOT BOATS HEADING OUT OF SWANSEA
Oil on canvas 62.7 × 89.2 cms
Collection of the National Library of Wales
Signed George Chambers 1836. Here is evidence of Chambers being in Swansea.
Harris is said to have worked in Chambers' studio.

George Chambers
SHIPPING OFF THE MUMBLES
Watercolour 19.3 × 29.5 cms
Collection of Mr. & Mrs. F. B. Cockett
Signed and dated 1838

# Edward Duncan RWS
## (1803-1882)

Edward Duncan RWS
OYSTER DREDGERS, SWANSEA BAY 1874
Watercolour 51.8 × 98.3 cms
Collection of the Glynn Vivian Art Gallery

Edward Duncan RWS
FISHING THE WEIR, SWANSEA
Watercolour 52 × 70 cms
Private Collection
Signed E. Duncan 1847. Exhibited Royal Watercolour Society 1847, no. 61.

Edward Duncan was born in Hampstead on October 20th 1803, the son of Thomas Duncan, a Scottish painter. He originally was trained as an Aquatint engraver by Robert Havill, but is best known as a prolific watercolour painter. In his early days he specialised in marine subjects. He married Bertha, daughter of W. J. Huggins, marine painter to King William IV. Duncan exhibited regularly in the London exhibitions and Graves' *Dictionary* lists him as showing a total of 558 works. He travelled extensively in Britain and on the Continent in search of subjects. From 1845 Swansea and Gower subjects appeared regularly until 1882, the year of his death, when he exhibited 'a Gower Cottage, Llanrhidian' at the Royal Watercolour Society. He died at Hampstead on April 11th 1882.

George Lance (1802–1864)
PORTRAIT OF
  EDWARD DUNCAN RWS
Oil on canvas 86.5 × 66.7 cms
Collection of the Royal Institution
of South Wales

Edward Duncan RWS
BOAT ON SHORE WITH OYSTER DREDGE,
  MUMBLES LIGHTHOUSE IN BACKGROUND
Pencil
Collection of Edward and Charles Harris
Signed E. Duncan, Oct 20th 1839, the first evidence of
Edward Duncan in South Wales.

*Opposite*
Edward Duncan RWS
WORMS HEAD FROM
  THE SEA
Pencil sketches 11 × 22/13.5 × 25 cms
Loaned by West Wales Antique Company
Both sketches bear Edward Duncan's
studio stamp.

The Worms Head
S. Wales

Edward Duncan RWS
OYSTER BOATS OFF MUMBLES
Watercolour 24 × 36 cms
Private Collection
Signed E. Duncan 1858

Edward Duncan RWS
WRECK OFF THE MUMBLES
Watercolour 20.5 × 33 cms
Collection of Dr. D. J. Harris
Signed 'Edward Duncan'

# The Reverend Calvert Richard Jones
## (1804-1877)

Calvert Richard Jones was born in 1804 at Veranda, a house still standing in Singleton Park, Swansea. In about 1813 the family moved to Heathfield House, near Mount Pleasant, and when his father died in 1847, Calvert Jones inherited his considerable wealth.

After Oriel College, Oxford, he took Holy Orders and in 1829 was installed as Rector of Loughor. An anonymous 'Reminiscences of Old Swansea' says of him that 'he never donned a surplice, but devoted himself to a splendid white pomeranian dog and to painting. His subjects were almost invariably shipping, not ships afloat, but lying high and dry in harbour or on the beach. Many were taken inside the piers, and I have watched the artist sitting there opposite his easel, in dangerous proximity to the mud'.

Calvert Jones was a close friend of C. R. M. Talbot of Margam, who was once described as 'the wealthiest commoner in Britain'. They were students at Oriel College together and Calvert Jones performed the marriage ceremony of Talbot to Lady Charlotte Butler in 1835. Talbot owned a series of steam yachts, the best known being 'The Lynx', in which he and his friends would cruise in the Mediterranean. The vessel was often based at Malta. Calvert Jones was a regular member of the party, and Mediterranean subjects are common in his work. Another advantage of his friendship was that Talbot was a cousin of Henry Fox Talbot of Laycock, the pioneer photographer, who had invented the calotype process, the first method of taking several positive images from a single negative. Fox Talbot guarded his interests in the calotype process by patents and the restriction of its use to those who were licensed by him.

Calvert Jones used the calotype process to record the ships and seamen in and around Swansea Harbour. These photographs are now highly prized and Calvert Jones is best known for this work. In addition to marine subjects he often produced figure studies drawn in pencil on tinted paper. These drawings are probably related to his photographic studies, as the subjects are always arranged in a pose with limbs supported, as was necessary with the long exposures required for photography. An exception to this is the white pomeranian dog, which must have been trained to keep still. Occasionally he worked in oil, usually not very effectively.

Calvert Jones was fond of making pencil and wash drawings of ship portraits. Many of these date from 1850-1860 at the time when steam power was replacing sail. It is an era of ship development which has not been fully studied, so that these records are an important and significant contribution.

The first public exhibition of Calvert Jones' work was held at the Glynn Vivian Art Gallery in 1973, and at that time he was completely unknown. Since then his work as an early photographer has been fully recognised, and the quality of his watercolour drawings is increasingly appreciated.

Calvert Jones was twice married and he had three daughters. Towards the end of his life he moved to Bath, and he died on March 7th 1879 at 11 Lansdowne Crescent. His body was brought back to Swansea and he was buried in the Cradock Chapel at St. Mary's Church.

Calvert R. Jones
MEN PULLING ON A ROPE
Pencil and bodycolour on tinted paper 15.2 × 25.5 cms
Private Collection

Calvert R. Jones
FAMILY GROUP AND DOG Sept 7 1846
Pencil and bodycolour on tinted paper 17.8 × 25.4 cms
Private Collection

PHOTOGRAPH OF CALVERT JONES
IN FAMILY GROUP WITH DOG
This may possibly be C. R. M. Talbot
With the permission of the Science Museum.

Calvert Jones' sketches are often related to photographs.
The subjects are supported to keep a pose for several
minutes.

Calvert R. Jones
PENCIL AND WATERCOLOUR DRAWINGS
FROM THE COLLECTION OF THE
GLYNN VIVIAN ART GALLERY
These are a selection from the Glynn Vivian's collection,
most of which were in the first exhibition of his work at the
Gallery in 1973.

Calvert R. Jones
SHIPPING IN HARBOUR
Pencil 19.7 × 26.7 cms
Collection of Colin and Janet Lacy

Calvert R. Jones
FIRING PRACTICE ON DECK
Pencil heightened with white 17.8 × 24.1 cms
Collection of Colin and Janet Lacy

Calvert R. Jones
FERRY-TREADMILL CONSTRUCTION
Pencil and wash 16.2 × 24.8 cms
Collection of Colin and Janet Lacy

Calvert R. Jones
COPIES OF EARLY
  CALOTYPE PHOTOGRAPHY
  SHOWING SUBJECTS
  AT SWANSEA *c*.1848
15.3 × 19.5 cms
By permission of the National Maritime Museum,
London.
Calvert Jones used Fox Talbot's calotype process
of photography, while working in and around
Swansea Harbour in 1840-50.

Calvert R. Jones Calotype Photography

# Henry B. Birchall
## (fl 1840-1850)

Henry B. Birchall
PILOT CUTTER TOM ROSSER *c.*1850
Oil on board 27 × 38 cms
Private Collection
Signed. Before 1860 as there is no battery around Mumbles lighthouse. Flies the white
ensign, which cannot be explained.

This unrecorded artist has left five or six marine subjects in oil, painted in 1840-1850 in the Swansea area.

Hunt's *Swansea Directory* of 1850 lists under the heading 'Artists',

       James Harris, Mumbles
       Henry Birchall, Bellvue Terrace
       W. Butler, Rutland Street

Pearce's *Swansea Directory* of 1854 lists Harris & Butler, only. Pearce's *Swansea Directory* of 1856 lists Henry Bath Birchall as Grocer and Tea Dealer at 15 Castle Square. Can this be the artist turned Grocer?

H. B. Birchall was in direct competition with James Harris as a marine artist, while W. Butler was a topographical artist.

Birchall's work is attractive, but not of the same class as James Harris and it is probable that he could not survive the competition as a professional artist.

The name Birchall recurs in the 1880-1890 when T. Birchall and T. Birchall, Junior, were two early members of the Swansea Art Society.

Henry B. Birchall
THREE MASTED SHIP OFF THE MUMBLES
Oil on canvas 34.5 × 53.5 cms
Private Collection
Signed. Date *c.*1845

Attributed to H. B. Birchall
SWANSEA PILOT BOATS *c.*1840-50
Oil on canvas 61 × 58 cms
Private Collection

Henry B. Birchall
SHIPPING IN SWANSEA BAY 1845
Oil on canvas 42.5 × 58.5 cms
Private Collection
Signed and dated

Attributed to H. B. Birchall
SHIPS WITH PILOT CUTTERS *c*.1840-50
Oil on canvas 46 × 84 cms
Private Collection

Attributed to H. B. Birchall
SHIPS WITH PILOT CUTTERS *c.*1840-1850
Oil on canvas 46 × 84 cms
Private Collection

# References

## General

*David Bell* 'The Artist in Wales' p. 180, Harrap 1957

*Peter J. Stuckey* 'The Sailing Pilots of the Bristol Channel' David and Charles 1977

*W. H. Jones* 'History of the Port of Swansea' W. Spurrel & Son, Carmarthen 1922

*N. L. Thomas* 'The Story of Swansea's Districts and Villages' The Guardian Press, Neath

*Gerald Gabb* 'The Story of the Village of Mumbles' D. Brown and Sons, Cowbridge 1986


## Harris Family

*Obituary* of James Harris Senior. The Cambrian Newspaper July 1st 1887

*Notice of 1902 Exhibition* and Biographical notes of Harris Family. The South Walian, December 1902, p. 186

*Catalogue* of the 14th Annual Exhibition of the Swansea Art Society, December 1902, including the catalogue of Harris Loan Exhibition

*History of the Swansea Art Society* 1886-1986

*The Mansel Papers* no. 954 Swansea Central Library

*W J Rogers* Harris and Calvert Jones pedigrees

## Calvert Jones

*Calvert R. Jones Exhibition* Catalogue Glynn Vivian Art Gallery 1973

*'Reminiscences of Old Swansea'* anon

## Edward Duncan

*The History of the Old Watercolour Society* J. L. Roger Longmans Green & Co. 1891

*Elis Jenkins* 'Convergence' Gower 1962, p. 29

*Frank L. Emanual* 'Edward Duncan RWS' Walker's Quarterly, October 1923

*Mrs. Hazel Giebel* Information on the Harris family

*Peter Ferguson* Information on Flags and Ship identification

*John Vivian Hughes* Information on C. R. M. Talbot

*Carl Smith* Information on wrecks and ship identification

We are indebted to the Council of the Royal Institution of South Wales (Swansea Museum) and to Miss Betty Nelmes, M.B.E., Administrator, for use of the Library facilities, and particularly information regarding the history of Swansea.

# Acknowledgements

We are very grateful to the many owners who have willingly loaned their paintings and so enabled a unique assembly of works for the exhibition.

'Under Sail' would never have been possible without the hard work and endeavours of Dr. Roderick Howell, both assiduously in researching the exhibition which has meant travelling the length and breadth of Britain and contributing the text which for the first time provides a context for the artists who were working in Swansea.

We are also indebted to all our sponsors who have generously supported this important publication for the City of Swansea, particularly Sir Leslie Joseph whose unerring support has been much appreciated.

Many people have assisted with this publication and a full reference list is included. I would also like to thank the Welsh Arts Council for their assistance with transporting the works and Roger Vlitos for taking the majority of the photos. A very special thank you is due to Bernice Keith for her capable organisation and management of all aspects of this publication and exhibition. Her fortitude has enabled the exhibition to take place.

Lastly but far from least, it is due to the support of the Leisure Services Committee and our own staff at the Glynn Vivian Art Gallery which has enabled the realisation of 'Under Sail'.

Hilary Woolley,
Director Swansea Museum Services.

The 'Under Sail' publication has been sponsored by many local individuals and companies.

We are particularly grateful to Sir Leslie Joseph for supporting the colour plates contained in this volume.

Other Sponsors whom we wish to thank are:

D. H. Andrews, Chartered Accountant, Swansea

Borg-Warner Ltd., Port Talbot, Glamorgan

Burgess & Company Ltd., Swansea

Courage Ltd., Wales Region

David Cross Gallery, 3A Boyces Ave., Clifton, Bristol

Philip Davies, Dealer in 19th/20th Century Pictures, Swansea

The South Wales Electricity Board

Fletchers of Port Talbot

John Francis, Fine Art Auctioneers, Carmarthen

Bernard Hastie & Co. Ltd., Swansea

Mr. & Mrs. Alistair Love

3M United Kingdom PLC

Morganite Electrical Carbon Ltd., Swansea

N. R. Omell, London

Phillips in Wales, Auctioneers, Cardiff

Thomas Thomas & Sons (Swansea) Ltd.

Jno. Oliver Watkins & Sons, Chartered Surveyors, Swansea

West Wales Antique Company, Murton, Swansea

James Harris
A MAN OF WAR AND OTHER VESSELS
OFF SWANSEA IN A BREEZE *c.*1865
Oil on board 14 × 24 cms
Collection of the National Library of Wales

# Swansea City Council
## Leisure Services Committee 1986/87

|  |  |
|---|---|
| *The Lord Mayor:* | Councillor L. M. Hopkin |
| *Chairman:* | Councillor A. Lloyd |
| *Vice-Chairman:* | Councillor G. Phillips |
|  | Councillor L. J. Aldron |
|  | Councillor H. W. Ayres |
|  | Councillor L. D. Bailey |
|  | Councillor C. Birss |
|  | Councillor P. M. Black |
|  | Councillor J. E. Burtonshaw |
|  | Councillor T. J. Exton |
|  | Councillor R. Francis-Davies |
|  | Councillor J. H. Guy |
|  | Councillor C. Hammacott |
|  | Councillor R. D. Lewis |
|  | Councillor R. J. Lloyd |
|  | Councillor P. F. MacDonald-Murray |
|  | Councillor H. J. Morgan |
|  | Councillor T. P. C. Morgan |
|  | Councillor J. T. G. Peters |
|  | Councillor C. L. Thomas |
|  | Councillor D. R. Watkins |